CATALOGUE OF DIGITIZED RARE SANSKRIT BUDDHIST MANUSCRIPTS

(Vol. 1: 1-200)

UNIVERSITY OF THE WEST

Rosemead, California, U.S.A.

Fall 2010

CATALOGUE OF DIGITIZED RARE SANSKRIT BUDDHIST MANUSCRIPTS

(Vol. 1: 1-200)

Edited by Miroj Shakya
Designed by Jesse Chang

Published by University of the West,
1409 N Walnut Grove Ave,
Rosemead, CA 91770, U.S.A.
Tel: (626) 571-8811
Fax: (626) 571-1413
E-mail: info@uwest.edu
Web site: www.uwest.edu

First Edition: 2010
ISBN: 978-0-9846002-0-5

Contents

Message from Venerable Master Hsing Yun 1

Message from President Dr. C.S. Wu 3

Foreword by Dr. Lewis Lancaster 5

Introduction by Miroj Shakya 7

Acknowledgement by Dr. Jue Ji 9

A Short History of Sanskrit Buddhist
Manuscripts by Min Bahadur Shakya 11

A Preliminary Handlist of Manuscripts 1-200
by Simharatna 16

Date, Author and Compiler Indexes 43

Title Index 44

Manuscript Samples 55

Message from Venerable Master Hsing Yun

It is my great pleasure to see the work on preservation of rare Sanskrit Buddhist Manuscripts launched by University of the West. These rare Sanskrit Buddhist Manuscripts are equally important as the *Pāli tripiṭaka* and Chinese *tripiṭaka*. The primary goal in my life is promoting Humanistic Buddhism through Buddhist culture, education, charity, and propagation of the Dharma. For more than four decades, Fo Guang Shan has been promoting projects like this, which combine modern technology with Buddhism and benefit all academics and students. I deeply believe that this digital version of rare Sanskrit Buddhist Manuscripts, along with this catalogue, will surely be very helpful to readers and potential users worldwide.

Venerable Master Hsing Yun
Founder,
University of the West,
Rosemead, California, U.S.A.
Fo Guang Shan Buddhist Order

Message from President Dr. C.S. Wu

I am glad to see this catalogue of the 200 digitized rare Sanskrit Buddhist Manuscripts from Kathmandu, Nepal, along with the digitized Manuscripts. These manuscripts are very rare and are valuable for researchers and students. We, the University of the West, are very proud to sponsor this project. I would like to thank all the staff and coordinator of this project for digitizing two hundred manuscripts in such a short period of time. This will remain an ongoing project. We are targeting to digitize one thousand manuscripts in the coming years. We will make this data available to the world free of charge.

Dr. C.S. Wu
President,
University of the West,
Rosemead, California, U.S.A.

Foreword

It is exciting to see the emergence of new "witnesses" for Sanskrit Buddhist texts. These scanned images provide us with beautiful color copies that come very close to giving the user the same experience as handling the physical manuscripts. I salute Venerable Master Hsing Yun and President Wu for the support they gave to this effort. Also, I express my appreciation for the staff in Kathmandu under the direction of Mr. Min Bahadur Shakya, who continues to produce such good results from their workshop. We all look forward to having hundreds of manuscript images available, free of charge, on the internet. It will be a major contribution to Buddhist Studies.

Dr. Lewis R. Lancaster
Director, ECAI, and Professor Emeritus,
University of California, Berkeley, California, U.S.A.

Founder,
Digital Sanskrit Buddhist Canon Project
University of the West,
Rosemead, California, U.S.A.

Introduction

It is a great pleasure to present a catalogue of Digitized Rare Sanskrit Buddhist Manuscripts facilitated by the University of the West, Rosemead, California, U.S.A. in collaboration with Nagarjuna Institute of Exact Methods (A Centre for Buddhist Studies), Nepal. This Digitized Collection comprises the scanned images of 200 Rare Sanskrit Buddhist Manuscripts in *Rañjanā*, *Pracalit*, and *Devanāgarī* scripts. This is an ongoing project and is still in the process of digitizing Buddhist texts.

The sources of these rare Sanskrit Buddhist manuscripts in digital form are Akṣeśvara Mahāvihāra and private collections of the Kathmandu Valley, most of which have not previously been digitized or microfilmed. Our goal is to scan these rare manuscripts and present the digital version of the manuscript to scholars and students free of charge. We hope that there will be substantial benefits for readers. We are planning to provide a descriptive catalogue of the Rare Sanskrit Buddhist Manuscripts in the near future.

Miroj Shakya
Project Coordinator,
Digital Sanskrit Buddhist Canon Project
Rare Sanskrit Buddhist Manuscript Preservation Project
University of the West,
Rosemead, California, U.S.A.

Acknowledgement

I would like to thank Venerable Master Hsing Yun for his kind support of this project, former President Dr. Allen Huang for initiating this project, and also express gratitude to Mr. Min Bahadur Shakya and his staff in Nepal, who have been sincerely working to scan all the images of these valuable manuscripts and to Simharatna for preparing this catalogue.

Special thanks are due to Akṣeśvara Mahāvihāra, Pulchok, Lalitpur, for allowing us to scan the entire manuscript collection from its library, and to all the personal collectors: Mr. Deepak Bajracharya, Mr. Sarvagya Ratna Bajracharya, the son of Pt. Ratnakaji Bajracharya, Mr. Yuga Ratna Shakya, and Mr. Puspa Raj Bajracharya, for entrusting us to scan their valuable manuscripts. I hope this booklet will be helpful for the reader.

Dr. Jue Ji
Supervisor,
Rare Sanskrit Buddhist Manuscript Preservation Project
Digital Sanskrit Buddhist Canon Project

Director,
Institute of Chinese Buddhist Studies
University of the West,
Rosemead, California, U.S.A.

A Short History of Sanskrit Buddhist Manuscripts

by Min Bahadur Shakya

We have come to know through our understanding of Buddhist history that an enormous amount of Buddhist literature was created in Sanskrit, beginning right after the Buddha's *Mahāparinirvāṇa*, continuing up to the 12th century AD in India. Out of this vast literature, comprising several thousand texts, only a portion was translated into Tibetan between the 7th and 15th centuries and into Chinese between the 2nd and 11th centuries. Unfortunately, with the passage of time, the great treasure of Buddhist literature in Sanskrit was lost or destroyed due to various developments over the course of history.

An exhaustive history of the Sanskrit Buddhist literature has long been needed. The reasons behind the scarcity of research into Sanskrit Buddhist literature are many. One of the major reasons is the disappearance of Buddhism from most of India and the unavailability of the original Sanskrit Buddhist works.

In 1824, Mr. Brian Hodgson, a British diplomat, discovered a great number of Sanskrit Buddhist manuscripts in Nepal and reported their existence to the modern world. The existence of these texts was unknown to the rest of the world before his time, and his discovery completely revolutionized the understanding of Buddhism among Europeans in the early part of the nineteenth century. Copies of these works, totaling 381 bundles of manuscripts, were distributed by Hodgson so as to render them accessible to European scholars.

Of these eighty-six manuscripts, comprising 179 separate works, many were presented to the Asiatic Society of Bengal; 85 went to the Royal Asiatic Society of London; 30 to the Indian Office Library; 7 to the Bodleian Library, Oxford; 174 to the Société Asiatique, and others reached French scholar Eugène Burnouf. The latter two collections have since been deposited in the Bibliothèque Nationale of

France.[1] With regard to the situation at this time, Prof. Jaya Deva Singh observes in his Introduction to Madhyamika Philosophy:

> Books on Mahayana Buddhism were completely lost in India. Their translations existed in Chinese, Japanese and Tibetan. Mahayana literature was written mostly in Sanskrit and mixed Sanskrit. Scholars who have made a study of Buddhism hardly suspected that there were also books on Buddhism in Sanskrit.

Similarly, Suniti Kumar Chatterji writes:

> One great service the people of Nepal did, particularly the highly civilized Newars of the Nepal Valley, was to preserve the manuscripts of Mahayana Buddhist literature in Sanskrit. It was the contribution of Sri Lanka to have preserved for humankind the entire mass of the Pali literature of Theravada Buddhism. This went also to Burma, Cambodia, and Siam. It was similarly the great achievement of the people of Nepal to have preserved the equally valuable original Sanskrit texts of Mahayana Buddhism.

It is therefore in Nepal that the vast majority of Sanskrit Buddhist documents have been preserved. Regarding the Buddhist literature circulating in Nepal, as many as 20 reports have been published.

Many of the manuscripts originally preserved in Nepal were carried out of the country by the pioneers of modern Indology. The earliest illustrated Manuscript of the *Aṣṭasāhasrikā Prajñāpāramitā*, dated 1015 A.D., is now in the collection of Cambridge University Library. This manuscript offered new and important material to students of South Asian and Central Asian art history. It is difficult to know exactly when the tradition of producing illustrated manuscripts began; but from available documents it seems that copying and writing such manuscripts began as early as the tenth century in Nepal, i.e. during Narendradeva's reign (998 A.D.).[2] Features of these manuscripts include miniatures and painted book covers.

---

1 See R.L.Mitra's *The Sanskrit Buddhist Literature of Nepal,* Calcutta (reprint) 1971, p.xxxv-vi.

2 See *Le Népal* by Prof. Sylvain Lévi. Here it is stated that on King Narendra Deva's deathbed, he seemed to have handed over two important things to his daughters: One is his own crown, and the other was a Manuscript of the *Prajñāpāramitā* scripture.

The special and characteristic peculiarity of Newar Buddhism is that its ritual and its sacred literature are written in the Sanskrit language, because of which we can call Newar Buddhism the only surviving form of "Sanskrit Buddhism". With the collapse of Buddhism in India, some Buddhists escaped from suppression and fled to Nepal. The Newars of the Kathmandu Valley accepted them and their religious and cultural inheritance. The two groups intermarried and their religions and cultures merged to become Newar Buddhism. This happened during a period from the 9th to the 13th century A.D. The Newars have continued to copy Sanskrit manuscripts up to the present day. All Buddhists owe a debt to the Newars, through whose efforts we have been able to study these Sanskrit manuscripts in the present day.

Types of Nepalese Manuscript Materials

Palm-leaf Manuscript [3]

Palm leaves are used for writing and painting because of their thin and flexible qualities. From the first millenium up to the 16th century, manuscripts were written on palm leaves called *Tādapatra.* Rolled palmleaf manuscripts are called *tāmsuks* and have been used mainly for legal deeds. At least 1084 rolled palmleaf manuscripts are held by the National Archives of Nepal alone. These were written from the 14th century onwards. One of the oldest among these dates from 1334 A.D.

Palm leaf provides an excellent surface for writing and can remain preserved in superb condition. It is usually safe from damage by worms and can be rolled into a small bundle for transport or storage. Most of these manuscripts extant in Nepal are written in *Bhujimol* script. Most of the historical documents of the early medieval period are found in these palm leaf texts. Rolled palm leaf manuscripts are often placed in small pigeonhole boxes made of straw board and bucrum. These boxes may then be stored inside a steel cabinet rack to protect them from dust, dirt and thieves.

---

3 See the article "Conservation of Rolled Palm Leaf Manuscripts (RPLM)" by Mr. Griha Man Singh in *"Abhilekha,"* published by The Nepal Archives, 1996.

Haritālika Paper Manuscript [4]

Haritālika or orpiment is yellow in color, has a crystalline structure, and is odorless, water-insoluble and impervious to inorganic salt. *Haritālika* is used to coat hand-made paper (Nepali paper) with some binding agent or medium to make it more durable and insect-resistant. Nepali hand-made papers are made from the bark of the *Loktā* plant, which contains sheets of a cellulose compound. It is creamy in color and usually contains small solid dark brown flecks due to the impurity of the pulp. Microscopic study of this paper clearly indicates that it contains long fibers, arranged irregularly, having a rough surface. Because of this, it offers a premium coating surface for *Haritālika* paste. The majority of hand-made papers are physically and chemically of good quality, high strength, and have a strong pH factor of 7-9. They have a high degree of tensile strength and folding endurance.

Thyāsaphū Paper Manuscript

These long rectangular folding books or leporellos are mainly employed in circumstances requiring ease of use, such as various rituals, *Dhāraṇī* recitation and the singing of *Stotra* or hymns.

Scroll Manuscript

This format is used most often for writing chronicles (*Vaṃśāvalīs*), or genealogical records of royal families.

Bound-Book Manuscript

Most bound-book manuscripts are relatively new, and were most probably imitations of Western examples.

Conclusion

The importance of putting these Sanskrit Buddhist texts into a digital format cannot be over-emphasized, for it is in these valuable Sanskrit documents that we have the original version of many of the Mahāyāna and Vajrayāna texts that were translated into the Chinese and Tibetan languages, and secondarily, into Korean, Japanese and Mongolian. The corpus of Sanskrit Buddhist literature

---

4 See the article "Haritālika coated envelope is a means of document preservation" by Mr. Griha Man Singh in *"Abhilekha"*, published by The Nepal Archives, 1994.

found in Nepal is comparable to the Pāli literature available today. It is imperative that these Sanskrit originals should be preserved in digital format so that they are accessible to researchers of all kinds.

Since the commencement of the Digital Sanskrit Buddhist Canon (DSBC) project at University of the West in the year 2003, we have received tremendous goodwill from scholars around the world about the worth and success of the project. In addition to the DSBC, starting from the inception of this Rare Buddhist Manuscript Preservation Project in March 2009, Nagarjuna Institute has scanned more than 200 titles of Manuscripts. collected from various monasteries and private collections. Our aim is to gather scans of the entire collection of Manuscripts (numbering more than 1000 titles) in collections which have not been digitized by previous efforts, such as those of the Nepal Research Center, Asha Archives and so on. This Rare Buddhist Manuscript Project will be a historic event in the field of digitizing world heritage.

Min Bahadur Shakya
Project Director,
Rare Sanskrit Buddhist Manuscript Preservation Project
Digital Sanskrit Buddhist Canon Project
Nagarjuna Institute of Exact Methods (A Centre for Buddhist Studies)
Chakupat, Lalitpur-10, Nepal

A Preliminary Handlist of Manuscripts 1-200 Digitized by the Rare Buddhist Manuscript Preservation Project

by Simharatna

Introduction

Manuscripts in Sanskrit are the primary means by which the ideas and traditions of pan-Indian Buddhism have been transmitted into the present day. Although many such manuscripts have been studied over the past two centuries, a great number, often containing unique information, still remain inaccessible. The following handlist of manuscripts digitized by the Rare Buddhist Manuscript Preservation Project (RBMPP) provides basic information about some of these previously unknown or undocumented manuscripts, which the RBMPP aims to make more widely available through digital photography.

The first two hundred manuscripts photographed by the RBMPP, described briefly in the following handlist, have been sourced from private collections in the Kathmandu Valley. It is here that the last surviving tradition of South Asian Mahayana, practiced by Buddhist Newars, still preserves and uses these texts. Several of the photographed manuscripts are kept in the collections of individuals such as Dīpak Vajrācārya and Puṣparāja Vajrācārya, and the late Ratnakājī Vajrācārya. The largest collection of manuscripts among those photographed belongs to the collection of a Newar Buddhist monastery, Akṣeśvara Mahāvihāra, located in Pulchowk, Patan, Nepal.

Several years ago, Akṣeśvara Mahāvihāra received bequests of manuscripts from the families of the late Śukrarāja Vajrācārya and Vācaspati Vajrācārya. These two gentlemen were members of the sangha of nearby Yaśodhara Mahāvihāra, also in Patan. Both collections of manuscripts have since been safely stored at Akṣeśvara Mahāvihāra, together with numbered title cards, which were created later and are referred to in the handlist. It is thought that part of Vācaspati Vajrācārya's collection was microfilmed by Ven. Shucho Takaoka in the 1970s; however, the digital images prepared by the RBMPP are richer and more detailed.

Thanks to the efforts of the RBMPP, working under the direction of Nagarjuna Institute in Patan, we are now able to access these valuable collections as digital scans. Their contents have been made available without depriving the owners of the originals. Hopefully other private and monastic collections, which are of such high importance for our understanding of South Asian Buddhism, can be opened up in the same way in the near future.

Manuscripts in these collections are almost always Buddhist in their content and affiliation. In addition, manuscript collections of Nepalese Buddhists sometimes contain works of wider interest belonging to the non-sectarian or secular tradition of Sanskritic learning. In the present collection, there are texts dealing with lexicography (Nos. 9, 168), medicine (Nos. 22, 58), astronomy/astrology (No. 96) and in two instances, with non-Buddhist tantra (Nos. 85, 200).

The following handlist of manuscript titles in the order is presented by the RBMPP. It provides titles, authors (if known), and information about the format of the manuscript, as well as the place of deposit and the date of writing, where available. The handlist is followed by indexes of dates, authors' names and titles in Roman and Devanagari. Certain features of some manuscripts, such as size and page counts, could not be verified at the time of writing (these are indicated with question marks); consequently, the handlist should be regarded as a provisional guide to the manuscripts digitized by the RBMPP to date, and as a stimulus to further research. A more detailed descriptive catalogue is currently under preparation.

Conventions

Titles
Wherever possible, titles in the handlist are taken directly from the colophons or preambles of manuscripts. As manuscripts are not always provided with unambiguous titles, where necessary titles have been devised for the purposes of compiling this handlist. Generic titles, which may be assigned to arbitrary compilations (*saṅgraha*) of hymns (*stotra*), tantric songs (*caryāgīta*) and so on, are indicated with brackets [ ]. Titles which have been devised according to the content of the manuscript, or which have been taken from some other source, are prefixed with an asterisk (*). The individual titles which make up such compilations, and the titles recorded on cards or covers attached to the manuscript, are not recorded in this short handlist.

Manuscript types
Several types of manuscripts are found in these collections; see Min Bahadur Shakya's article for a description of these manuscript types. The term "folding book" corresponds to Newar *thyāsaphū*. Manuscript sizes are only mentioned if they have so far been recorded (in either centimetres or inches) by the digitization staff of the RBMPP.

Script
Three types of script (*lipi*) are found in these manuscripts: *Rañjanā*, *Pracalita*, and *Devanāgarī*, the former two being used only in Nepal. More than one script may appear in the same manuscript.

Language
Manuscripts which include ritual instructions, rubrics or other interspersed text in the Newar language are described as "Sanskrit and Newar." Translations into Newar are noted as such. Tibetan is also sometimes encountered in these manuscripts. The Sanskritic language of the *caryāgīta* compilations is routinely described as Sanskrit, although these compilations often use unusual forms of Sanskrit, or other Indic languages.

Date
Dates recorded in the manuscripts are normally Nepal *Samvat* (NS), corresponding to 879–880 CE, or *Vikram Samvat* (VS).

N.B.: Certain details of individual manuscripts, such as numbers of folios, could not be directly verified at the time of writing, and such uncertainties are indicated where possible with "(?)" marks.

Format

(number): (title) (author). (material), (folio count and pagination), (lines per page), (width and height), (script), (language(s)). (place of deposit and collection number). (date).

Catalogue

1: *Acalābhiśekavidhi.* Unbound paper, 58 folios, 16 lines/page, complete, Pracalita script, Sanskrit and Newar. Akṣeśvara Mahāvihāra collection No. 9. Dated NS 1020. Illustrated.

2: *Acalābhiṣekavidhi.* Folding book, 24 folios, 5 lines/page, 23.8 × 8.5 cm., complete, Pracalita script, Sanskrit and Newar. collection of Ratnakājī Vajrācārya.

3: **Acalābhiṣekavidhi.* Folding book, 20 folios, 6 lines/page, complete, Pracalita script, Sanskrit. Akṣeśvara Mahāvihāra (Śukrarāja Vajrācārya collection) No. 28. Dated NS 1020.

4: **Ācāryaguṭhīvidhi.* Folding book, 44 folios(?), 6 lines/page, complete, Pracalita script, Sanskrit and Newar. Akṣeśvara Mahāvihāra (Vācaspati Vajrācārya collection) No. 69.

5: **Ācāryābhiṣekavidhi.* Bound book, 18 folios(?), 14 lines/page, 10.5 × 18.3 cm., complete, Pracalita script, Sanskrit and Newar. Akṣeśvara Mahāvihāra (Śukrarāja Vajrācārya collection) No. 96(166). Dated NS 1045.

6: *Kriyāsaṅgraha* by Kuladatta. Unbound paper, 179 folios, 6–8 lines/page, 33.3 × 9 cm., complete, Pracalita script, Sanskrit. Ratnakājī Vajrācārya collection. Dated NS 1104.

7: **Ahorātrayajña.* Folding book, 23(?) folios, 5 lines/page, complete, Pracalita script, Sanskrit and Newar. Akṣeśvara Mahāvihāra collection. Dated NS 923.

8: *Ahorātrayajña.* Folding book, 12 folios(?), 6–7 lines/page, complete, Pracalita script, Sanskrit and Newar. Akṣeśvara Mahāvihāra collection No. 145.

9: *Amarakoṣa.* Unbound paper, 170 folios, 5 lines/page, complete, Devanagari script, Sanskrit and Newar (translation). Akṣeśvara Mahāvihāra (Vācaspati Vajrācārya collection) No. 63. Dated NS 1012.

10: **Piṇḍadānārcana*. Folding book, 58 folios, 6 lines/page, complete, Pracalita script, Sanskrit and Newar. Akṣeśvara Mahāvihāra (Vācaspati Vajrācārya collection) No. 19. Dated NS 1070.

11: *Mañjuśrīnāmasaṅgīti*. Folding book, 16 folios, 17 lines/page, complete, Rañjanā script, Sanskrit. Akṣeśvara Mahāvihāra (Śukrarāja Vajrācārya collection) No.170.

12: [*Stotrasaṅgraha*]. Bound book, 20 folios, 17–19 lines/page, complete, Devanagari script, Sanskrit. Akṣeśvara Mahāvihāra (Śukrarāja Vajrācārya collection) No.118.

13: *Pañcaviṃśatisahasrikāprajñāpāramitā*. Unbound paper, 543 folios, 9 lines/page, complete, Pracalita script, Sanskrit.

14: *Pañcarakṣā*. Unbound paper, 142 folios, 6–7 lines/page, 27.7 × 8.5 cm., complete, Pracalita script, Sanskrit. collection of Ratnakājī Vajrācārya.

15: *Mañjuśrīnāmasaṅgīti*. Unbound paper, 26 folios, 5 lines/page, 8.7 × 2.8 cm., complete, Pracalita script, Sanskrit. Puṣparāja Vajrācārya collection. Dated NS 1025.

16: *Rātridigpūjā*. Bound book, 10 folios, 10 lines/page, complete, Pracalita script, Sanskrit. Akṣeśvara Mahāvihāra collection No. 140.

17: **Aṣṭamīvratavidhi*. Unbound paper, 18 folios, 12 lines/page, complete, Devanagari script, Sanskrit and Newar. Akṣeśvara Mahāvihāra (Śukrarāja Vajrācārya collection) No. 184. Undated.

18: **Amoghapāśalokeśvarapūjāvidhi*. Folding book, 56 folios, 6 lines/page, complete, Pracalita script, Sanskrit. Akṣeśvara Mahāvihāra (Śukrarāja Vajrācārya collection) No. 22. Illustrated.

19: **Aṣṭamīvratakathā*. Unbound paper, 170 folios, 6–8 lines/page, 10 × 3.12in complete, Pracalita script, Newar language. Ratnakājī Vajrācārya collection (in the possession of Sarvajñaratna). Dated (date uncertain; "vasubānanatdrāstī").

20: *Bālagrahaśāntī*. Bound book, 12 folios (numbered 1–22), 11 lines/page, complete, Devanagari script, Sanskrit and Newar. Akṣeśvara Mahāvihāra collection No. 121.

21: [*Stotrasaṅgraha*]. Folding book, 18 folios, 5 lines/page, complete(?), Devanagari script, Sanskrit. Akṣeśvara Mahāvihāra collection.

22: *Bhīmavinodacikitsā* by Dāmodara. Unbound paper, 378 folios, 8–9 lines/page, complete, Devanagari script, Sanskrit. Akṣeśvara Mahāvihāra collection(?) No. 19.

23: *Bhīmarathakriyā*. Bound book, 11 folios, 17 lines/page, complete, Devanagari script, Sanskrit and Newar. Akṣeśvara Mahāvihāra (Śukrarāja Vajrācārya collection) No. 90.

24: *Bhīmarathāvarārohaṇakarma*. Folding book, 39 folios, 6 lines/page, complete, Pracalita script, Sanskrit. Akṣeśvara Mahāvihāra No. 2.

25: *Bodhicaryāvatāra*. Unbound paper, 47 folios, 8 lines/page, complete, Pracalita script, Sanskrit. Ratnakājī Vajrācārya collection (? in the possession of Sarvajñaratna). Dated NS 959.

26: *Bodhicaryāvatārapañjikā* (ch.9) by Prajñākaramati. Bound book, 48 folios, 23 lines/page, Devanagari script, Sanskrit and Newar (translation). Akṣeśvara Mahāvihāra (Śukrarāja Vajrācārya collection) No. 168.

27: *Bodhicaryāvatārapañjikā* (ch.9) by Prajñākaramati. Continues from no.27. Bound book, 12(?) folios, 28 lines/page, complete, Devanagari script, Sanskrit and Newar (translation by Ratnabahādur Vajrācārya). Akṣeśvara Mahāvihāra (Śukrarāja Vajrācārya collection) No. 84.

28: *Avadānaśataka.* Unbound paper, 298 folios, 9 lines/page, 32.8 × 13 cm., complete, Pracalita script, Sanskrit. Akṣeśvara Mahāvihāra (Vācaspati Vajrācārya collection) No. 16.

29: *Svayaṃbhūpurāṇoddhṛtabuddhagīta.* Bound book, 8 folios, 12 lines/page, complete, Devanagari script, Sanskrit. Akṣeśvara Mahāvihāra collection No. 127.

30: [*Stotrasaṅgraha*]. Bound book, 8 folios, 12 lines/page, complete, Devanagari script, Sanskrit. Akṣeśvara Mahāvihāra (Śukrarāja Vajrācārya collection) No. 120.

31: *Buddhagīta.* Bound book, 10 folios, 8 lines/page, complete, Devanagari script, Sanskrit. Akṣeśvara Mahāvihāra (Śukrarāja Vajrācārya collection) No. 92.

32: [*Caryāgītasaṅgraha*]. Printed, 84 folios, 6–8 lines/page, 23.2 × 7.8? cm., complete, Pracalita script, Sanskrit. Akṣeśvara Mahāvihāra collection No. 69(136).

33: *Cacāsaphū saṃgraha* compiled by Badrīratna Vajrācārya. Printed, 9 folios (numbered 1–18), 5 lines/page, complete, Devanagari script, Sanskrit. Akṣeśvara Mahāvihāra collection No. 177 (donated by the Satvapūjā khalaḥ, Mantrasiddhi Mahāvihāra, Kathmandu). Undated.

34: *Caṇḍamahāroṣaṇamukhākhyana.* Folding book, 19 folios, 6 lines/page, complete, Pracalita script, Sanskrit. Akṣeśvara Mahāvihāra (Śukrarāja Vajrācārya collection) No. 92. Dated NS 1069.

35: *Caṇḍamahāroṣaṇatantra.* Folding book, 63 folios, 6 lines/page, 13 × 4 in., complete, Pracalita script, Sanskrit. Akṣeśvara Mahāvihāra (Vācaspati Vajrācārya collection) No. 36.

36: [*Caryāgītasaṅgraha*]. Folding book, 50 folios, 6 lines/page, Pracalita script, Sanskrit. Akṣeśvara Mahāvihāra (Śukrarāja Vajrācārya collection) No. 14.

37: [*Caryāgītasaṅgraha*]. Folding book, 20 folios, 6 lines/page, complete(?), Devanagari script, Sanskrit. Akṣeśvara Mahāvihāra collection No. 41.

38: [*Caryāgītasaṅgraha*]. Folding book, 14(?) folios, 6 lines/page, complete, Pracalita script, Sanskrit. Akṣeśvara Mahāvihāra collection No. 73. Dated NS 920.

39: [*Caryāgītasaṅgraha*]. Folding book, 4 folios, 6 lines/page, incomplete, Devanagari script, Sanskrit. Akṣeśvara Mahāvihāra collection No. 63.

40: [*Caryāgītasaṅgraha*]. Folding book, 35 folios, 6 lines/page, complete, Pracalita script, Sanskrit. Akṣeśvara Mahāvihāra (Vācaspati Vajrācārya collection?) No. 43.

41: [*Caryāgītasaṅgraha*]. Folding book, 54 folios, 7 lines/page, complete, Pracalita script, Sanskrit. Akṣeśvara Mahāvihāra (Śukrarāja Vajrācārya collection) No. 3.

42: [*Caryāgītasaṅgraha*]. Folding book, 11 folios, 5 lines/page, complete, Pracalita script, Sanskrit. Akṣeśvara Mahāvihāra (Śukrarāja Vajrācārya collection) No. 71.

43: [*Caryāgītasaṅgraha*]. Folding book, 11 folios, 5 lines/page, complete, Pracalita script, Sanskrit. Akṣeśvara Mahāvihāra (Śukrarāja Vajrācārya collection) No. 58.

44: [*Caryāgītasaṅgraha*]. Folding book, 4 folios, 6 lines/page, complete, Pracalita script, Sanskrit. Akṣeśvara Mahāvihāra (Śukrarāja Vajrācārya collection) No. 48.

45: [*Caryāgītasaṅgraha*]. Folding book, 20 folios, 8–9 lines/page, complete, Pracalita script, Sanskrit. Akṣeśvara Mahāvihāra (Śukrarāja Vajrācārya collection) No. 33. Dated NS 1053.

46: [*Caryāgītasaṅgraha*]. Folding book, 36 folios, 8 lines/page, complete(?), Pracalita script, Sanskrit.

47: [*Caryāgītasaṅgraha*]. Folding book, 20 folios, 5 lines/page, complete, Pracalita script, Sanskrit. Akṣeśvara Mahāvihāra collection No. 68.

48: [*Caryāgītasaṅgraha*]. Folding book, 19(?) folios, 7 lines/page, incomplete, Pracalita script, Sanskrit. Akṣeśvara Mahāvihāra (Śukrarāja Vajrācārya collection) No. 21.

49: [*Caryāgītasaṅgraha*]. Folding book, 16(?) folios, 5 lines/page, complete, Pracalita script, Sanskrit. Akṣeśvara Mahāvihāra collection No. 35.

50: [*Caryāgītasaṅgraha*]. Bound book, 7 folios, 8–10 lines/page, complete, Devanagari script, Sanskrit. Akṣeśvara Mahāvihāra (Śukrarāja Vajrācārya collection). Dated VS 2036.

51a: *Catuṣpīṭhatantra*. Unbound paper, 77 folios, 6 lines/page, complete, Pracalita script, Sanskrit. Dated NS 1028. Illustrated.
51b: [*Catuṣpīṭhamaṇḍalopāyikā*]. Unbound paper, 55 folios (numbered 78–130), 6 lines/page, complete, Pracalita script, Sanskrit. Illustrated.
51c: *Catuṣpīṭhanibandha by* Bhavabhaṭṭa. Unbound paper, 174 folios (numbered 131–304), 6 lines/page, complete, Pracalita script, Sanskrit. Illustrated.
51d: *Dhūmāṅgarīsādhāna*. Unbound paper, 1 folio, 6 lines/page, complete, Pracalita script, Sanskrit. Illustrated. Akṣeśvara Mahāvihāra (Vācaspati Vajrācārya collection) No. 51.

52: See No. 51.

53: *Catuḥṣaṣṭibalipūjā*. Folding book, 43 folios, 60 lines/page, 20.3 × 9.5 cm., complete, Pracalita script, Sanskrit and Newar. Akṣeśvara Mahāvihāra No. 38.

54: **Catuḥṣaṣṭibalividhi*. Folding book, 42(?) folios, 8 lines/page, 24 × 11 cm., complete, Pracalita script, Sanskrit and Newar. Akṣeśvara Mahāvihāra No. 32.

55: *Cūḍākarmasaṃkṣiptavidhi*. Folding book, 22 folios, 8 lines/page, complete, Pracalita script, Sanskrit and Newar. Akṣeśvara Mahāvihāra (Śukrarāja Vajrācārya collection) No. 60.

56: *Pravrajyāvratacūḍākarmavidhi*. Bound book, 32 folios, 13 lines/page, complete, Devanagari script, Sanskrit and Newar. Akṣeśvara Mahāvihāra (Śukrarāja Vajrācārya collection) No. 149.

57a: *Bhīmarathāvarārohaṇakarma*. Folding book, 9 folios, 5–6 lines/page, complete, Pracalita script, Sanskrit and Newar.
57b: **Cūḍākarmavidhi*. Folding book, 13 folios (numbered 10–23), 5–6 lines/page, complete, Pracalita script, Sanskrit and Newar.
Akṣeśvara Mahāvihāra collection No. 81. Dated NS 950.

58: *Nidānacikitsā*. Unbound paper, 247 folios, 7 lines/page, 12 × 4 in., incomplete, Pracalita script, Sanskrit and Newar. Akṣeśvara Mahāvihāra (Vācaspati Vajrācārya collection) No. 42.

59: *Dānaṃ gomaya gāthā* by Nāgārjuna. Folding book, 5 folios, 8 lines/page, complete, Devanagari script, Sanskrit. Akṣeśvara Mahāvihāra (Śukrarāja Vajrācārya collection) No. 42.

60: *Daśakarmapratiṣṭhākriyāvidhi*. Folding book, 28 folios, 6–7 lines/page, complete, Pracalita script, Sanskrit and Newar. Akṣeśvara Mahāvihāra collection No. 13.

61: **Daśakarmavidhi*. Folding book, 36(?) folios, 6 lines/page, 9.7 × 4 cm., complete(?), Pracalita script, Sanskrit and Newar. Dīpak Vajrācārya collection.

62: *Daśākuśalapāpadeśanā*. Unbound paper, 3 folios, 5 lines/page, Pracalita script, Sanskrit. Akṣeśvara Mahāvihāra (Śukrarāja Vajrācārya collection) No. 160.

63: **Daśamīpūjāvidhi*. Folding book, 16(?) folios, 5–6 lines/page, complete, Pracalita script, Sanskrit and Newar. Akṣeśvara Mahāvihāra (Śukrarāja Vajrācārya collection) No. 70. Dated NS 855.

64: *Ṣaṭpāramitāstotra*. Bound book, 4 folios, 13 lines/page, complete, Devanagari script, Sanskrit. Akṣeśvara Mahāvihāra (Śukrarāja Vajrācārya collection) No. 96.

65: [*Jīrṇoddhāradevadevīpūjā*]. Bound book, 32(?) folios, 12 lines/page, complete, Pracalita script, Sanskrit and Newar. Akṣeśvara Mahāvihāra (Śukrarāja Vajrācārya collection) No. 103.

66: *Dhāraṇīsaṅgraha*. Unbound paper, 20 folios, 5 lines/page, Pracalita script, Sanskrit and Newar. Akṣeśvara Mahāvihāra (Śukrarāja Vajrācārya collection?) No. 74. Dated NS 1085.

67: [*Dhāraṇīsaṅgraha*]. Bound book, 14 folios (numbered 17–21), complete, Devanagari script, Sanskrit. Akṣeśvara Mahāvihāra (Śukrarāja Vajrācārya collection) No. 96.

68: **Dhūmāṅgārīpūjāvidhi*. Bound book, 3 folios, 6–9 lines/page, 6 × 4 in., complete, Devanagari script, Sanskrit and Newar. Akṣeśvara Mahāvihāra (Śukrarāja Vajrācārya collection) No. 86.

69: **Dhūmāṅgārīpūjāvidhi*. Bound book, 12 folios, 15 lines/page, complete, Pracalita script, Sanskrit and Newar. Akṣeśvara Mahāvihāra (Śukrarāja Vajrācārya collection) No. 86.

70: [*Caryāgītasaṅgraha*]. Folding book, 54 folios, 8–9 lines/page, complete, Pracalita & Devanagari script, Sanskrit. Akṣeśvara Mahāvihāra (Śukrarāja Vajrācārya collection) No. 9.

71: **Dīkṣāvidhi*. Folding book, 64 folios, 7 lines/page, 22.5 × 8.9 cm., complete, Pracalita script, Sanskrit and Newar. Collection of Ratnakājī Vajrācārya. Dated NS 880.

72a: *Divyāvadāna.* Unbound paper, 396 folios (1–396v), 12 lines/page, complete, Devanagari script, Sanskrit.
72b: *Ahorātravratacaityasevānuśaṃśāvadāna.* Unbound paper, 13 folios (numbered 396–408), 12 lines/page, complete, Devanagari script, Sanskrit.
Akṣeśvara Mahāvihāra (Vācaspati Vajrācārya collection) No. 11. Dated NS 908.

73: *Durgatipariśodhana.* Unbound paper, 110 folios, 5 lines/page, 3 × 10 in., complete, Pracalita script, Sanskrit.
Akṣeśvara Mahāvihāra collection No. 41.

74: *Durgatimaṇḍalapūjā.* Bound book, 33(?) folios, 12 lines/page, complete, Devanagari script, Sanskrit and Newar. Akṣeśvara Mahāvihāra (Śukrarāja Vajrācārya collection) No. 34.

75: **Durgatipariśodhanamaṇḍalapratiṣṭhāvidhi.* Unbound paper, 16 folios, 6–7 lines/page, complete, Pracalita script, Sanskrit and Newar. Akṣeśvara Mahāvihāra collection No. 56.

76a: *Dvādaśatīrthasnānavidhi.* Unbound paper, 6 folios, 9 lines/page, complete, Pracalita script, Sanskrit.
76b: *Śākyasiṃhastotra.* Unbound paper, 3 folios, 9 lines/page, complete, Pracalita script, Sanskrit.
Akṣeśvara Mahāvihāra collection No. 132.

77: *Dvādaśatīrthamāhātmya.* Exercise book, 36 folios (numbered 1–78), 25–26 lines/page, complete, Pracalita script, Newar language. Akṣeśvara Mahāvihāra (Śukrarāja Vajrācārya collection) No. 11.

78: *Dvādaśatīrthamāhātmya.* Unbound paper, 59 folios, 5–6 lines/page, 23.3 × 8.4 cm., complete, Devanagari script, Sanskrit. Ratnakājī Vajrācārya collection (in the possession of Sarvajñaratna). Dated VS 2027.

79: *Dvādaśatīrthe piṇḍakriyā.* Bound book, 16(?) folios, 16 lines/page, complete, Pracalita & Devanagari script,Sanskrit and Newar. Akṣeśvara Mahāvihāra (Śukrarāja Vajrācārya collection) No. 113.

80: *Dvādaśatīrthe piṇḍakriyā.* Bound book, 18(?) folios, 11 lines/page, complete, Devanagari script, Sanskrit and Newar. Akṣeśvara Mahāvihāra (Śukrarāja Vajrācārya collection) No. 113. This is a copy of No.79.

81: *Dvādaśatīrthasnānavidhi.* Bound book, 3 folios, 6 lines/page, complete, Pracalita script, Newar language. Akṣeśvara Mahāvihāra (Śukrarāja Vajrācārya collection) No. 38.

82: *Grahamātṛkādhāraṇī.* Unbound paper, 15 folios, 5 lines/page, complete, Devanagari script, Sanskrit. Akṣeśvara Mahāvihāra (Śukrarāja Vajrācārya collection) No. 82.

83: [*Āśīrvāda*]. Unbound paper, 3 folios, 7 lines/page, complete(?), Pracalita script, Sanskrit. Akṣeśvara Mahāvihāra collection No. 159.

84: **Guhyakalaśapūjā.* Folding book, 18(?) folios, 7 lines/page, complete(?), Devanagari script, Sanskrit and Newar. Akṣeśvara Mahāvihāra collection No. 39(?).

85: *Guhyakālītantra* (part) and others. Folding book, 43 folios, 12 lines/page, complete(?), Pracalita script, Sanskrit. Illustrated.

86: **Guhyalokottaratantra.* Bound book, 16 folios, 18–20 lines/page, complete, Devanagari script, Sanskrit and Newar. Akṣeśvara Mahāvihāra (Śukrarāja Vajrācārya collection) No. 167.

87: [*Guhyamantrapūjā*]. Bound book, 34(?) folios, 10 lines/page, complete, Pracalita script, Sanskrit and Newar. Akṣeśvara Mahāvihāra collection No. 99. Illustrated.

88: **Guhyapiṇḍakriyā.* Folding book, 15 folios (numbered 1–30), 8 lines/page, 10.3 × 23.3 cm., complete(?), Devanagari script, Sanskrit and Newar. Akṣeśvara Mahāvihāra collection No. 17.

89: *Sampuṭatantra* (chapters 15–20). Bound book, 16 folios, 22 lines/page, complete, Devanagari script, Sanskrit. Akṣeśvara Mahāvihāra (Śukrarāja Vajrācārya collection) No. 169.

90: *Guhyasamājatantra.* Unbound paper, 168 folios, 5 lines/page, complete, Pracalita script, Sanskrit. Ratnakājī Vajrācārya collection (in the possession of Sarvajñaratna). Dated NS 830. Illustrated.

91: *Kāraṇḍavyuha.* Unbound paper, 116 folios, 5 lines/page, complete, Pracalita script, Sanskrit. Akṣeśvara Mahāvihāra (Vācaspati Vajrācārya collection) No. 58. Dated NS 939 NS (according to the date on the cover).

92: *Kāraṇḍavyuha.* See No.58.

93a: *Kolāsyasindhūrārcanasaṃkṣiptapūjā.* Folding book, 23 folios, 5 lines/page, complete, Pracalita script, Sanskrit and Newar.
93b: *Hevajranairātmāpūjā.* Folding book, 21 folios, 5 lines/page, complete, Pracalita script, Sanskrit and Newar.

94: *Yantrayā rakṣā.* Folding book, 24 folios, 6 lines/page, complete(?), Pracalita script, Sanskrit and Newar. Akṣeśvara Mahāvihāra collection No. 75.

95: **Jātakarmavidhi.* Unbound paper, 16 folios, 9 lines/page, complete, Devanagari script, Sanskrit. Akṣeśvara Mahāvihāra (Śukrarāja Vajrācārya collection) No. 129.

96: *Jyotiṣasārapañjikā* by Śrījīvadatta. Unbound paper, 105 folios, 5 lines/page, complete, Devanagari script, Sanskrit and Newar. Akṣeśvara Mahāvihāra (Vācaspati Vajrācārya collection) No. 6.

97: *Kāraṇḍavyūha.* Unbound paper, 66 folios, 9 lines/page, complete, Pracalita script, Sanskrit. Akṣeśvara Mahāvihāra (Vācaspati Vajrācārya collection) No. 52. Illustrated.

98a: *Āryatārānāmāṣṭottaraśataka.* Unbound paper, 9 folios, 6 lines/page, incomplete, Pracalita script, Sanskrit.
98b: *Karuṇāstava* by Bandhudatta. Unbound paper, 15 folios, 6 lines/page, complete, Pracalita script, Newar language. Akṣeśvara Mahāvihāra (Śukrarāja Vajrācārya collection) No. 31.

99: *Caturdaśābhiṣekavidhi.* Folding book, 34 folios, 7 lines/page, complete, Pracalita script, Sanskrit and Newar. Akṣeśvara Mahāvihāra collection No. 15.

100: *Kriyāsaṅgraha* by Kuladatta. Unbound paper, 236 folios, 6 lines/page, complete, Pracalita script, Sanskrit. Akṣeśvara Mahāvihāra (Vācaspati Vajrācārya collection) No. 23. Dated NS 1023.

101: *Kriyāsaṅgraha* by Kuladatta. Unbound paper, 222 folios (1–193, 294–322), 6 lines/page, complete, Devanagari script, Sanskrit. Akṣeśvara Mahāvihāra (Śukrarāja Vajrācārya collection) No. 23. Dated VS 2038.

102: *Adbhutakuladīpadharmarājakathā* by Vikramānanda. Printed, 98 folios, 9 lines/page, 25 × 13 cm., complete, Devanagari script, Sanskrit. Ratnakājī Vajrācārya collection (in the possession of Sarvajñaratna) No.9. Dated NS 1035.

103: *Saṃkṣiptalakṣacaityaracitavratavidhi.* Folding book, 23 folios, 5 lines/page, complete, Pracalita script, Sanskrit and Newar. Akṣeśvara Mahāvihāra (Śukrarāja Vajrācārya collection?) No. 42.

104: *Sugatajanmaratnāvadānamālā.* Unbound paper, 394 folios, 9–15 lines/page, 12 × 6 in., complete, Pracalita & Devanagari script,Sanskrit. Akṣeśvara Mahāvihāra (Vācaspati Vajrācārya collection) No. 12.

105: *Laṅkāvatārasūtra.* Unbound paper, 219 folios, 5 lines/page, 12 × 4 in., complete, Pracalita script, Sanskrit. Akṣeśvara Mahāvihāra collection No. 14. Dated NS 918.

106: *Kāraṇḍavyūha* (ch.1–12). Unbound paper, 43 folios, (numbered 10–63), 5 lines/page, incomplete, Pracalita script, Sanskrit. Akṣeśvara Mahāvihāra collection No. 21.

107: **Mahābalikriyā.* Folding book, 26 folios, (numbered 1–50), 6 lines/page, 24 × 10.3 cm., complete, Pracalita script, Sanskrit and Newar. Ratnakājī Vajrācārya collection No. [10].

108: [*Pūjāpaddhati*]. Folding book, 18 folios, 6–8 lines/page, complete, Pracalita script, Sanskrit and Newar. Akṣeśvara Mahāvihāra collection No. 51.

109: *Mahāmeghamahāyānasūtra* (chapters 64–65). Unbound paper, 45 folios, 6 lines/page, complete, Pracalita script, Sanskrit. Akṣeśvara Mahāvihāra collection No. 67.

110: *Sukhāvatīvyūhamahāyānasūtra.* Unbound paper, 35 folios, 5 lines/page, incomplete, Devanagari script, Sanskrit. Akṣeśvara Mahāvihāra (Śukrarāja Vajrācārya collection) No. 135.

111: *Mahāyānasūtrālaṃkāra.* Unbound paper, 155 folios, 7 lines/page, complete, Pracalita script, Sanskrit. Akṣeśvara Mahāvihāra (Vācaspati Vajrācārya collection) No. 40. Dated NS 1015.

112a: [unidentified]. Unbound paper, 24 folios, 7 lines/page, 12 × 4 in., complete(?), Pracalita script, Sanskrit.
112b: *Durgatipariśodhanatantra* (?). Unbound paper, 7 lines/page, Pracalita script, Sanskrit.
112c: *Mañjuśrī pārājikā* (?). Unbound paper, 7 lines/page, Pracalita script, Sanskrit.
Akṣeśvara Mahāvihāra (Śukrarāja Vajrācārya collection) No. 46.

113: [*Mantradhāraṇī*]. Unbound paper, 32 folios, 5–8 lines/page, complete, Pracalita & Devanagari script,Sanskrit. Akṣeśvara Mahāvihāra (Śukrarāja Vajrācārya collection) No. 72. Illustrated.

114: *Tattvajñānasaṃsiddhipañjikā Marmakālikā by* Vīryaśrīmitra (mantroddhara chapter). Unbound paper, 6 folios, 6 lines/page, complete, Pracalita script, Sanskrit. Akṣeśvara Mahāvihāra collection No. 161. Illustrated.

115: *Mañjuśrīnāmasaṅgīti.* Folding book, 28 folios, 8 lines/page, complete, Devanagari script, Sanskrit. Akṣeśvara Mahāvihāra (Śukrarāja Vajrācārya collection) No. 156.

116: *Mañjuśrīnāmasaṅgīti.* Unbound paper, 7 folios, 5 lines/page, incomplete, Devanagari script, Sanskrit. Akṣeśvara Mahāvihāra (Śukrarāja Vajrācārya collection) No. 162.

117: *Ṅodo śāstra.* 137 folios: printed (21v–22r, 37v–137v) and handwritten paper (1–21r, 22v–37r), 9 lines/page, complete, Devanagari script, Tibetan and Newar (translation). Akṣeśvara Mahāvihāra (Śukrarāja Vajrācārya collection) No. 38. Dated NS 1073.

118: *Nityācāravidhi.* Bound book, 12 folios, 14 lines/page, complete, Devanagari script, Sanskrit and Newar. Akṣeśvara Mahāvihāra (Śukrarāja Vajrācārya collection) No. 108.

119: *Pañcābhiṣekavidhi.* Unbound paper, 31 folios (numbered 1–27, 1–4), 6 lines/page, 20.5 × 8.5 cm., complete, Pracalita script, Sanskrit and Newar, collection of Ratnakājī Vajrācārya. Dated NS 978.

120: **Pañcarakṣāpūjāvidhi.* Folding book, 34 folios, 6 lines/page, complete, Pracalita script, Sanskrit and Newar. Akṣeśvara Mahāvihāra collection No. 52.

121: *Pañcarakṣā.* Unbound paper, 93 folios, 5 lines/page, 24.1 × 8 cm., complete, Devanagari script, Sanskrit and Newar. collection of Ratnakājī Vajrācārya (? in the possession of Sarvajñaratna). Dated NS 1016. Illustrated.

122a: *Mahāmeghamahāyānasūtra.* Unbound paper, 42 folios, 6–7 lines/page, 13 × 3in complete, Pracalita script, Sanskrit.
122b: Pañcarakṣā. Unbound paper 8 folios (numbered 104–111), 6–7 lines/page, 13 × 3 in., incomplete, Pracalita script, Sanskrit. Akṣeśvara Mahāvihāra collection No. 73.

123: *Pāpaparimocana.* Unbound paper, 22 folios, 7 lines/page, complete, Devanagari script, Sanskrit. Akṣeśvara Mahāvihāra (Śukrarāja Vajrācārya collection) No. 24. Dated NS 1107.

124: *Phalānnaprāśanavidhi.* Folding book, 12(?) folios, 5–6 lines/page, complete, Devanagari script, Sanskrit and Newar. Akṣeśvara Mahāvihāra (Śukrarāja Vajrācārya collection) No. 137.

125: *Ṣoḍaśapiṇḍavidhi*. Folding book, 34 folios, 5–6 lines/page, complete, Pracalita script, Sanskrit and Newar. Akṣeśvara Mahāvihāra (Śukrarāja Vajrācārya collection) No. 55. Dated NS 1108.

126: [*Piṇḍakriyāvidhi*]. Folding book, 30 folios, 7 lines/page, complete, Pracalita script, Sanskrit and Newar. Akṣeśvara Mahāvihāra (Śukrarāja Vajrācārya collection) No. 44.

127: [*Piṇḍakriyāvidhi*]. Folding book, 44 folios, 6 lines/page, complete, Devanagari script, Sanskrit and Newar. Akṣeśvara Mahāvihāra (Śukrarāja Vajrācārya collection) No. 50. Dated NS 1073.

128: [*Piṇḍakriyāvidhi*]. Folding book, 27 folios, 6 lines/page, complete, Devanagari script, Sanskrit and Newar. Akṣeśvara Mahāvihāra (Śukrarāja Vajrācārya collection) No. 138.

129: *Prajñāpāramitāstotra* by Rāhulabhadra. Bound book, 5 folios, 15 lines/page, complete, Devanagari script, Sanskrit and Newar (translation). Akṣeśvara Mahāvihāra (Śukrarāja Vajrācārya collection).

130a: *Prajñopāyaviniścayasiddhi* by Anaṅgavajra. Bound book, 20 folios (1–20), 11–13 lines/page, complete, Devanagari script, Sanskrit.
130b: *Jñānasiddhi* by Indrabhūti. Bound book, 54 folios (21–74), 11–13 lines/page, complete, Devanagari script, Sanskrit. Akṣeśvara Mahāvihāra (Śukrarāja Vajrācārya collection) No. 133. This MS is probably copied from Bhattacharyya's printed text.[1]

131a: *Mahāpratyaṅgirāmahāvidyārājñī*. Folding book, 22 folios, 7 lines/page, complete, Devanagari script, Sanskrit.
131b: Āryatārānāmāṣṭottaraśatakaṃ. 7 lines/page, complete, Devanagari script, Sanskrit. Akṣeśvara Mahāvihāra (Śukrarāja Vajrācārya collection) No. 54.

---

1 Benoytosh Bhattacharrya (ed.) *Two Vajrayāna Works*. Gaekwad's Oriental Series, No 44. Baroda: Oriental Institute, 1929.

132: *Sitātapatrānāmāparājitāmahāvidyārājñī.* Unbound paper, 21 folios, 5 lines/page, 20.5 × 6.8 cm., complete, Pracalita script, Sanskrit. Ratnakājī Vajrācārya collection.

133: **Rañjanālipi.* Bound book, 15 folios, 4–7 lines/page, complete, Rañjanā script, Sanskrit. Akṣeśvara Mahāvihāra (Śukrarāja Vajrācārya collection) No. 116.

134: **Ratnanyāsāvidhi.* Bound book, 14 folios, 16 lines/page, complete, Devanagari script, Sanskrit. Akṣeśvara Mahāvihāra (Śukrarāja Vajrācārya collection) No. 88.

135: *Rātripūjā.* Bound book, 14(?) folios, 12 lines/page, complete, Pracalita script, Sanskrit. Akṣeśvara Mahāvihāra (Śukrarāja Vajrācārya collection?) No. 148.

136: *Sahasrāhutiyajñavidhi.* Folding book, 21(?) folios, 20 lines/page, complete, Pracalita script, Sanskrit and Newar. Akṣeśvara Mahāvihāra collection. Dated NS 918. Illustrated.

137: **Samādhi.* Folding book, 21 folios (numbered 1–34, [1–4]), 14.3 × 7.8 cm., complete, Sanskrit and Newar. collection of Ratnakājī Vajrācārya. Dated NS 1069.

138: *Saṃkṣiptabauddhastotrasaṅgraha* compiled by Dharmaharṣa Vajrācārya. Printed 14 folios, 11 lines/page, complete, Devanagari script, Sanskrit. Akṣeśvara Mahāvihāra (Śukrarāja Vajrācārya collection) No. 119. Dated NS 1060 & 1064.

139: **Saṃkṣiptabodhicittotpāda.* Bound book, 4 folios, 9 lines/page, complete, Devanagari script, Sanskrit and Newar. Akṣeśvara Mahāvihāra (Śukrarāja Vajrācārya collection) No. 144. Dated VS 2051.

140: **Saṃkṣiptaguhyapūjā.* Unbound paper, 80(?) folios, 9–12 lines/page, 10 × 7 in., complete, Pracalita script, Sanskrit and Newar. Akṣeśvara Mahāvihāra (Vācaspati Vajrācārya collection) No. 61.

141: **Saṃkṣiptakriyāvidhi*. Bound book, 40 folios, 16 lines/page, incomplete, Devanagari script, Sanskrit and Newar. Akṣeśvara Mahāvihāra collection No. 94.

142: [*Stotrasaṅgraha*]. Bound book, 4 folios, 12 lines/page, complete, Pracalita script, Sanskrit. Akṣeśvara Mahāvihāra (Śukrarāja Vajrācārya collection) No. 112.

143: *Samvarodayatantra*. Unbound paper, 79 folios, 7 lines/page, complete, Pracalita script, Sanskrit. Akṣeśvara Mahāvihāra collection No. 78.

144: **Samyakdānapūjāvidhi*. Folding book, 13 folios, 6 lines/page, complete, Pracalita script, Sanskrit and Newar. Akṣeśvara Mahāvihāra collection No. 99. Dated NS 1012. Illustrated.

145: **Samyakdānarājanimantraṇavidhi*. Folding book, 8(?) folios, 5 lines/page, complete, Pracalita script, Sanskrit and Newar. Akṣeśvara Mahāvihāra (Śukrarāja Vajrācārya collection) No. 105.

146: *Śāntikamaṇḍalāgniyajñavidhāna*. Folding book, 27 folios, 5–18 lines/page, complete(?), Pracalita script, Sanskrit and Newar. Akṣeśvara Mahāvihāra (Śukrarāja Vajrācārya collection) No. 97/146.

147: *Sindūrārohanapūjā*. Folding book, 24(?) folios, 5 lines/page, complete, Pracalita script, Sanskrit and Newar. Akṣeśvara Mahāvihāra (Vācaspati Vajrācārya collection) No. 99.

148: *Sindūrārohanapūjāvidhi*. Folding book, 70 folios, 7 lines/page, complete(?), Pracalita script, Sanskrit and Newar. Akṣeśvara Mahāvihāra collection No. 131.

149: *Sindūrapūjāvidhi*. photocopy 14 folios, 6 lines/page, 35.3 × 25 cm., complete, Pracalita script, Sanskrit and Newar. Akṣeśvara Mahāvihāra (Śukrarāja Vajrācārya collection). Dated NS 1023.

150: *Saṃkṣiptapiṇḍakriyā.* Folding book, 42(?) folios, 5 lines/page, complete, Pracalita script, Sanskrit and Newar. Akṣeśvara Mahāvihāra collection No. 139. Dated NS 996.

151: **(śrī)Aṣṭamātṛkāyajñabalividhi.* Folding book, 50(?) folios, 7–17 lines/page, complete, Pracalita script, Sanskrit and Newar. Akṣeśvara Mahāvihāra collection No. 65.
Dated NS 8??.

152: *(śrī)Mahāmaṇḍaleśvaradarśaṇa.* Folding book, 16 folios, 5–7 lines/page, complete, Pracalita script, Sanskrit. Akṣeśvara Mahāvihāra collection No. 61.

153: **(śrī)Cakrasamvaramūladikṣāvidhi.* Folding book, 97(?) folios, 6 lines/page, incomplete, Pracalita script, Sanskrit and Newar. Akṣeśvara Mahāvihāra (Śukrarāja Vajrācārya collection) No. 1.

154: *(śrī)Cakrasamvarapūjāvidhi.* Folding book, 12 folios, 6–7 lines/page, complete, Pracalita script, Sanskrit. Akṣeśvara Mahāvihāra (Śukrarāja Vajrācārya collection?)
No. 80. Dated NS 1054.

155: *(śrī)Mahāmaṇḍaleśvaradarśaṇa.* Folding book, 30 folios, 6 lines/page, complete(?), Pracalita script, Sanskrit. Akṣeśvara Mahāvihāra (Śukrarāja Vajrācārya collection) No. 23.

156: **Acalābhiṣekavidhi.* Folding book, 24(?) folios, 5 lines/page, 8.5 × 21.5 cm., complete, Pracalita script, Sanskrit. Akṣeśvara Mahāvihāra (Śukrarāja Vajrācārya collection) No. 24.

157: *(śrī)Candramahāroṣaṇatantra.* Unbound paper, 10(?) folios, 9 lines/page, 23.5 × 13.5 cm., complete, Devanagari script, Sanskrit. Akṣeśvara Mahāvihāra (Śukrarāja Vajrācārya collection) No. 154.

158: **Acalābhiṣekavidhi.* Unbound paper, 13(?) folios, 7 lines/page, complete, Pracalita script, Sanskrit. Akṣeśvara Mahāvihāra (Śukrarāja Vajrācārya collection) No. 26.

159: *Dharmadhātuvāgīśvaramaṇḍaladhyāna.* Folding book, 37 folios, 6 lines/page, complete, Pracalita script, Sanskrit. Akṣeśvara Mahāvihāra collection No. 53.

160: *Samvarodayatantra.* Unbound paper, 100 folios, 6 lines/page, 23.5 × 8.3 complete, Pracalita script, Sanskrit. Ratnakājī Vajrācārya collection (? in the possession of Sarvajñaratna). Dated NS 925.

161: [*Stotrasaṅgraha*]. Bound book, 16(?) folios, 14 lines/page, complete, Devanagari script, Sanskrit. Akṣeśvara Mahāvihāra (Śukrarāja Vajrācārya collection) No. 93.

162: *Āryatārānāmāṣṭottaraśataka.* Folding book, 6 folios, 6 lines/page, complete, Rañjanā script, Sanskrit. Akṣeśvara Mahāvihāra collection No. 104.

163: *Vajradhātumukhākhyāna.* Folding book, 38 folios, 8–10 lines/page, complete, Pracalita script, Sanskrit. Akṣeśvara Mahāvihāra collection No. 10. Dated NS 897. Illustrated.

164: **Vajravārāhīsamādhi.* Bound book, 15 folios, 9 lines/page, complete(?), Pracalita script, Sanskrit. Ratnakājī Vajrācārya collection No. 10.

165: **Vajravārāhīyogavidhi.* Unbound paper, 14(?) folios, 6 lines/page, complete, Pracalita script, Newar language. Akṣeśvara Mahāvihāra collection No. 57.

166: *(śrī)Vasudhārādhāraṇī.* Unbound paper, 19 folios, 6 lines/page, complete, Pracalita script, Sanskrit. Akṣeśvara Mahāvihāra (Śukrarāja Vajrācārya collection) No. 37.

167: *Pūjāpaddhati.* Folding book, 48(?) folios, 7 lines/page, complete, Pracalita script, Sanskrit and Newar. Akṣeśvara Mahāvihāra collection No.19.

168a: *Śrutabodha* by Kālidāsa. Unbound paper, 5 folios, 7 lines/page, complete, Pracalita script, Sanskrit.

168b: *Dhanañjayakośa* by Dhanañjaya. Unbound paper, 10 folios, 5 lines/page, Devanagari script, Sanskrit with Newar glosses. Akṣeśvara Mahāvihāra collection No.175.

169: [*Stotrasaṅgraha*]. Bound book, 21(?) folios, 14 lines/page, complete(?), Pracalita & Rañjanā script, Sanskrit. Akṣeśvara Mahāvihāra (Śukrarāja Vajrācārya collection) No. 110.

170: [*Stotrasaṅgraha*]. Bound book, 2 folios, 8–9 lines/page, 6 × 4 in., complete, Devanagari script, Sanskrit. Akṣeśvara Mahāvihāra (Śukrarāja Vajrācārya collection) No. 185.

171: [*Stotrasaṅgraha*]. Bound book, 116 folios (1–229), 15–16 lines/page, complete, Devanagari script, Sanskrit. Akṣeśvara Mahāvihāra collection No. 130. Undated. With index.

172: [*Stotrasaṅgraha*]. Bound book, 6 folios, 16 lines/page, unfinished, Devanagari script, Sanskrit. Akṣeśvara Mahāvihāra (Śukrarāja Vajrācārya collection) No. 122.

173: [*Stotrasaṅgraha*]. Bound book, 59 folios, 10 lines/page, complete, Devanagari script, Sanskrit. Akṣeśvara Mahāvihāra (Śukrarāja Vajrācārya collection) No. 142(147). Dated VS 2003.

174: [*Stotramantrasaṃgraha*]. Folding book, 17 folios, 7 lines/page, 6.6 × 3.82 cm., complete, Sanskrit and Newar. Puṣparāja Vajrācārya collection.

175: [*Stotrasaṅgraha*]. stitched 18 folios, 7 lines/page, 9.5 × 3.7 cm., complete, Pracalita script, Sanskrit. NIEM collection. Dated NS 797.

176: *Sukhāvatīvyūha.* Unbound paper, 80 folios, 5 lines/page, 13 × 3.5 in., complete, Pracalita script, Sanskrit. Akṣeśvara Mahāvihāra (Vācaspati Vajrācārya collection) No. 45. Dated NS 931.

177: *Sūryapūjāvidhi.* Bound book, 15 folios, 5 lines/page, complete, Devanagari script, Sanskrit and Newar. Akṣeśvara Mahāvihāra (Śukrarāja Vajrācārya collection) No. 147.

178: *Suvarṇaprabhāsottamasūtra.* Unbound paper, 137 folios, 5 lines/page, 13.1 × 8.3 cm., complete, Pracalita script, Sanskrit. Dīpak Vajrācārya collection. Dated NS 878. Illustrated.

179: *Suvarṇaprabhāsottamasūtra.* Unbound paper, 92 folios (numbered 1–27,1–12,1–12,1–7,1–11,1–12,1–12), 7 lines/page, complete, Pracalita script, Sanskrit. Akṣeśvara Mahāvihāra (Vācaspati Vajrācārya collection) No. 25. Illustrated.

180: *Suvarṇaprabhāsottamasūtra.* Unbound paper, 115+1 folios, 6 lines/page, 12 × 4 in., complete, Pracalita script, Sanskrit. Akṣeśvara Mahāvihāra (Vācaspati Vajrācārya collection) No. 53. Dated NS 971.

181: *Suvikrāntavikrāmiparipṛcchā Prajñāpāramitā* (ch.1). Unbound paper, 31 folios, 6 lines/page, complete, Pracalita script, Sanskrit. Akṣeśvara Mahāvihāra (Śukrarāja Vajrācārya collection) No. 41. (Note: This manuscript was probably copied from Vaidya's published text.)

182: *(Dīrgha)Sindūrārcanapūjā.* Unbound paper, 40(?) folios, 8 lines/page, complete, Pracalita script, Sanskrit and Newar. Akṣeśvara Mahāvihāra (Vācaspati Vajrācārya collection) No. 65. Dated NS 915.

183: *(Mahā)Sindūrārcanavidhi.* Unbound paper, 21 folios, 6 lines/page, 21.7 × 8.7 cm., complete, Pracalita script, Sanskrit and Newar. Ratnakājī Vajrācārya collection No. 28. Dated NS 995.

184: *Saptaśatasahasrādipūjā.* Unbound paper, 12 folios (numbered 1–24), 20 lines/page, complete, Pracalita script, Sanskrit. Akṣeśvara Mahāvihāra collection No. 166. Dated VS 2028.

185: *Tārāpārajikā.* Bound book, 10 folios, 19 lines/page, complete, Devanagari script, Sanskrit. Akṣeśvara Mahāvihāra (Śukrarāja Vajrācārya collection) No. 150.

186: *Āryatārānāmāṣṭottaraśataka.* Bound book, 22(?) folios, 14 lines/page, complete, Devanagari script, in Sanskrit, Tibetan and Newar (translation). Akṣeśvara Mahāvihāra collection No. 123.

187: [*Dhāraṇīstotrasaṅgraha*]. Bound book, 20 folios, 10 lines/page, complete, Devanagari script, Sanskrit. Akṣeśvara Mahāvihāra collection No. 171.

188: *Tārāvratavidhi*. Bound book, 28(?) folios, 12–14 lines/page, complete, Devanagari script, Sanskrit and Newar. Akṣeśvara Mahāvihāra (Śukrarāja Vajrācārya collection) No. 115.

189: *Tripañcaśatakalaśacihnasthāpanakramavidhi*. Folding book, 20 folios, 5 lines/page, complete, Pracalita script, Sanskrit. Akṣeśvara Mahāvihāra collection No. 78. Dated NS 793. Illustrated.

190: **Nityapūjāvidhi*. Exercise book, 58 folios, 7–9 lines/page, 10 × 16.5 cm., complete, Devanagari script, Sanskrit and Newar (translation). Akṣeśvara Mahāvihāra (Śukrarāja Vajrācārya collection) No. 134.

191: *Ugratārāsamādhi*. Folding book, 10(?) folios, 7 lines/page, complete, Pracalita script, Sanskrit and Newar. Akṣeśvara Mahāvihāra collection No. 77. Dated NS 932.

192: *Antyeṣṭikriyāvidhi*. Folding book, 66(?) folios, 6 lines/page, complete, Pracalita script, Sanskrit and Newar. Akṣeśvara Mahāvihāra (Vācaspati Vajrācārya collection?) No. 40.

193: *Upoṣadhavratavidhi*. Folding book, 62(?) folios, 7 lines/page, 21.4 × 10.4 cm., complete, Devanagari script, Sanskrit and Newar. Akṣeśvara Mahāvihāra (Śukrarāja Vajrācārya collection) No. 45.

194: *Utkrāntikriyāvidhi*. Bound book, 11 folios, 14 lines/page, complete, Pracalita script, Sanskrit and Newar. Akṣeśvara Mahāvihāra (Vācaspati Vajrācārya collection?) No. 89.

195: *Vajravārāhī degulī*. Folding book, 10 folios, 5 lines/page, 18.5 × 8 cm., complete, Pracalita script, Sanskrit and Newar. collection of Ratnakājī Vajrācārya.

196: *Vajravārāhīmaṇḍalapūjā*. Bound book, 10+1 folios, 11 lines/page, complete, Pracalita script, Sanskrit. Akṣeśvara Mahāvihāra collection No. 114.

197: *Pāpaparimocana.* Unbound paper, 44(?) folios, 7 lines/page, 29 × 12 cm., complete, Devanagari script, Sanskrit and Newar (translation). Ratnakājī Vajrācārya collection (in the possession of Sarvajñaratna). Dated VS 1986.

198: *Vīrakuśāvadāna.* Folding book, 70 folios (4r–74v), 6 lines/page, incomplete, Pracalita script, Sanskrit and Newar (translation). Akṣeśvara Mahāvihāra (Śukrarāja Vajrācārya collection) No. 163.

199: **Yajñavidhi.* Folding book, 32 folios, 6 lines/page, incomplete, Pracalita script, Sanskrit and Newar. Akṣeśvara Mahāvihāra collection No. 64.

200: *Yoginīvijayastava.* Bound book, 30(?) folios, 13 lines/page, complete, Devanagari script, Sanskrit. Akṣeśvara Mahāvihāra (Śukrarāja Vajrācārya collection?) No. 97.

Dates Index

(NS)

793	189	959	25	1064	138
797	175	971	180	1069	34, 137
830	90	978	119	1070	10
855	63	995	183	1073	127
878	178	996	150	1085	66
880	71	1012	9, 144	1104	6
897	163	1015	111	1107	123
8??	151	1016	121	1108	125
915	182	1020	1, 3	(?)	19
918	105, 136	1023	100, 149	VS 1986	197
920	38	1025	15	VS 2003	173
923	7	1028	51	VS 2027	78
925	160	1035	102	VS 2028	184
931	176	1045	5	VS 2036	50
939	91	1053	45	VS 2038	101
950	57	1054	154	VS 2051	139

Authors Index

Anangavajra 130a
Bandhudatta 98b
Bhavabhaṭṭa 51c
Dāmodara 22
Dhanañjaya 168b
Indrabhūti 130b
Kālidāsa 168b
Kuladatta 6, 100, 101
Nāgārjuna 59
Prajñākaramati 26, 27
Rāhulabhadra 129
Śrījīvadatta 96
Vikramānanda 102
Vīryaśrīmitra 114

Compilers Index

Badrīratna Vajrācārya 33
Dharmaharṣa Vajrācārya 138

Titles Index in Roman

Acalābhiśekavidhi	1, 2, 3, 156, 158
Ācāryābhiṣekavidhi	5
Ācāryaguṭhīvidhi	4
Adbhutakuladīpadharmarājakathā	102
Ahorātravratacaityasevānuśaṁśāvadāna	72b
Ahorātrayajña	7, 8
Amarakoṣa	9
Amoghapāśalokeśvarapūjāvidhi	18
Antyeṣṭikriyāvidhi	192
Āryatārānāmāṣṭottaraśataka	98a, 131b, 162, 186
[Āśīrvāda]	83
Aṣṭamātṛkāyajñabalividhi	151
Aṣṭamīvratakathā	19
Aṣṭamīvratavidhi	17
Avadānaśataka	28
Bālagrahaśāntī	20
Bhīmarathakriyā	23
Bhīmarathāvarārohaṇakarma	24, 57a
Bhīmavinodacikitsā	22
Bodhicaryāvatāra	25
Bodhicaryāvatārapañjikā	26–27
Buddhagīta	31
Cacāsaphū saṁgraha	33
[Cakrasamvara]mahāmaṇḍaleśvaradarśaṇa	152, 155
Cakrasamvaramūladikṣāvidhi	153
Cakrasamvarapūjāvidhi	154
Caṇḍamahāroṣaṇamukhākhyana	34
Caṇḍamahāroṣaṇatantra	35, 157
[Caryāgītasaṁgraha]	32, (33,) 36, 37, 38, 39, 40, 41, 42, 43, 44, 45, 46, 47, 48, 49, 50, 70
Catuḥṣaṣṭibalipūjā	53
Catuḥṣaṣṭibalividhi	54
Caturdaśābhiṣekavidhi	99

Catuṣpīṭhamaṇḍalopāyikā	51b
Catuṣpīṭhanibandha	51c
Catuṣpīṭhatantra	51a
Cūḍākarmasaṁkṣiptavidhi	55
Cūḍākarmavidhi	57b
Dānagomayagāthā	59
Daśakarmapratiṣṭhākriyāvidhi	60
Daśakarmavidhi	61
Daśākuśalapāpadeśanā	62
Daśamīpūjāvidhi	63
Dhanañjayakośa	168b
[Dhāraṇīsaṁgraha]	66, 67
[Dhāraṇīstotrasaṁgraha]	187
Dharmadhātuvāgīśvaramaṇḍaladhyāna	159
Dhūmāṅgārīpūjāvidhi	68, 69
Dhūmāṅgarīsādhāna	51d
Dīkṣāvidhi	71
Dīrghasindūrārcanapūjā	182
Divyāvadāna	72a
Durgatimaṇḍalapūjā	74
Durgatipariśodhana	73
Durgatipariśodhanamaṇḍalapratiṣṭhāvidhi	75
Durgatipariśodhanatantra	112b
Dvādaśatīrthamāhātmya	77, 78
Dvādaśatīrthasnānavidhi	76a, 81
Dvādaśatīrthe piṇḍakriyā	79, 80
Grahamātṛkādhāraṇī	82
Guhyakalaśapūjā	84
Guhyakālītantra	85
Guhyalokottaratantra	86
Guhyamantrapūjā	87
Guhyapiṇḍakriyā	88
Guhyasamājatantra	90
Hevajranairātmyāpūjā	93b
Jātakarmavidhi	95

Jīrṇoddhāradevadevīpūjā	65
Jñānasiddhi	130b
Jyotiṣasārapañjikā	96
Kāraṇḍavyuha	91, 92, 97, 106
Karuṇāstava	98b
Kolāsyasindhūrārcanasaṁkṣiptapūjā	93a
Kriyāsaṁgraha	6, 100, 101
Laṅkāvatārasūtra	105
Mahābalikriyā	107
Mahāmaṇḍaleśvaradarśaṇa	152, 155
Mahāmeghamahāyānasūtra	109, 122a
Mahāpratyaṅgirāmahāvidyārājñī	131a
Mahāsindūrārcanavidhi	183
Mahāyānasūtrālaṁkāra	111
Mañjuśrīnāmasaṅgīti	11, 15, 115, 116
Mañjuśrīpārājikā (?)	112c
[Mantradhāraṇī]	113
Nidānacikitsā	58
Nityācāravidhi	118
Nityapūjāvidhi	190
Ṅodo śāstra	117
Pañcābhiṣekavidhi	119
Pañcarakṣā	14, 121, 122b
Pañcarakṣāpūjāvidhi	120
Pañcaviṁśatisahasrikāprajñāpāramitā	13
Pāpaparimocana	123, 197
Phalānnaprāśanavidhi	124
Piṇḍadānārcana	10
[Piṇḍakriyāvidhi]	126, 127, 128
Prajñāpāramitāstotra	129
Prajñopāyaviniścayasiddhi	130a
Pravrajyāvratacūḍākarmavidhi	56
Pūjāpaddhati	167, 108
Rañjanālipi	133
Ratnanyāsāvidhi	134

Rātridigpūjā 16
Rātripūjā 135
Sahasrāhutiyajñavidhi 136
Śākyasiṁhastotra 76b
Samādhi 137
Saṁkṣiptabauddhastotrasaṁgraha 138
Saṁkṣiptabodhicittotpāda 139
Saṁkṣiptaguhyapūjā 140
Saṁkṣiptakriyāvidhi 141
Saṁkṣiptalakṣacaityaracitavratavidhi 103
Saṁkṣiptapiṇḍakriyā 150
Sampuṭatantra 89
Samvarodayatantra 143, 160
Samyakdānapūjāvidhi 144
Samyakdānarājanimantraṇavidhi 145
Śāntikamaṇḍalāgniyajñavidhāna 146
Saptaśatasahasrādipūjā 184
Ṣaṭpāramitāstotra 64
Sindūrapūjāvidhi 149
Sindūrārohanapūjā 147
Sindūrārohanapūjāvidhi 148
Sitātapatrānāmāparājitāmahāvidyārājñī 132
Ṣoḍaśapiṇḍavidhi 125
Śrutabodha 168a
[Stotramantrasaṁgraha] 174
[Stotrasaṁgraha] 12, 21, 30, 142, 161, 169, 170, 171, 172, 173, 175
Sugatajanmaratnāvadānamālā 104
Sukhāvatīvyūha 176
Sukhāvatīvyūhamahāyānasūtra 110
Sūryapūjāvidhi 177
Suvarṇaprabhāsottamasūtra 178, 179, 180
Suvikrāntavikrāmiparipṛcchā prajñāpāramitā 181
Svayaṁbhūpurāṇoddhṛtabuddhagīta 29
Tārāpārajikā 185
Tārāvratavidhi 188

Tattvajñānasaṁsiddhipañjikā marmakālikā	114
Tripañcaśatakalaśacihnasthāpanakramavidhi	189
Ugratārāsamādhi	191
Upoṣadhavratavidhi	193
Utkrāntikriyāvidhi	194
Vajradhātumukhākhyāna	163
Vajravārāhī degulī	195
Vajravārāhīmaṇḍalapūjā	196
Vajravārāhīsamādhi	164
[Vajravārāhīyogavidhi]	165
Vasudhārādhāraṇī	166
Vīrakuśāvadāna	198
Yajñavidhi	199
Yantrayā rakṣā	94
Yoginīvijayastava	200

Titles Index in Devanagari

अचलाभिशेकविधि	1, 2, 3, 156, 158
अद्भुतकुलदीपधर्मराजकथा	102
अन्त्येष्टिक्रियाविधि	192
अमरकोष	9
अमोघपाशलोकेश्वरपूजाविधि	18
अवदानशतक	28
अष्टमातृकायज्ञबलिविधि	151
अष्टमीव्रतकथा	19
अष्टमीव्रतविधि	17
अहोरात्रयज्ञ	7, 8
अहोरात्रव्रतचैत्यसेवानुशंशावदान	72b
आचार्यगुठीविधि	4
आचार्याभिषेकविधि	5
आर्यतारानामाष्टोत्तरशतक	98a, 131b, 162, 186
[आशीर्वाद]	83
उग्रतारासमाधि	191
उत्क्रान्तिक्रियाविधि	194
उपोषधव्रतविधि	193
करुणास्तव	98b
कारण्डव्युह	91, 92, 97, 106
कोलास्यसिन्धूरार्चनसंक्षिप्तपूजा	93a
क्रियासंग्रह	6, 100, 101
गुह्यकलशपूजा	84
गुह्यकालीतन्त्र	85
गुह्यपिण्डक्रिया	88
गुह्यमन्त्रपूजा	87
गुह्यलोकोत्तरतन्त्र	86

गुह्यसमाजतन्त्र	90
ग्रहमातृकाधारणी	82
ङोदो शास्त्र	117
चक्रसम्वरपूजाविधि	154
[चक्रसम्वर]महामण्डलेश्वरदर्शन	152, 155
चक्रसम्वरमूलदिक्षाविधि	153
चचासफू संग्रह	33
चण्डमहारोषणतन्त्र	35, 157
चण्डमहारोषणमुखाख्यन	34
चतुर्दशाभिषेकविधि	99
चतुःषष्टिबलिपूजा	53
चतुःषष्टिबलिविधि	54
चतुष्पीठमण्डलोपायिका	51b
चतुष्पीठतन्त्र	51a
चतुष्पीठनिबन्ध	51c
[चर्यागीतसंग्रह]	32, (33,) 36, 37, 38, 39,40, 41, 42, 43, 44, 45,46, 47, 48, 49, 50, 70
चूडाकर्मविधि	57b
चूडाकर्मसंक्षिप्तविधि	55
जातकर्मविधि	95
जीर्णोद्धारदेवदेवीपूजा	65
ज्ञानसिद्धि	130b
ज्योतिषसारपञ्जिका	96
तत्वज्ञानसंसिद्धिपञ्जिका मर्मकालिका	114
तारापारजिका	185
ताराव्रतविधि	188
त्रिपञ्चशतकलशचिह्नस्थापनक्रमविधि	189
दशकर्मप्रतिष्ठाक्रियाविधि	60
दशकर्मविधि	61
दशमीपूजाविधि	63

दशाकुशलपापदेशना	62
दानगोमयगाथा	59
दिव्यावदान	72a
दीक्षाविधि	71
दीर्घसिन्दूरार्चनपूजा	182
दुर्गतिपरिशोधन	73
दुर्गतिपरिशोधनतन्त्र	112b
दुर्गतिपरिशोधनमण्डलप्रतिष्ठाविधि	75
दुर्गतिमण्डलपूजा	74
द्वादशतीर्थमाहात्म्य	77, 78
द्वादशतीर्थस्नानविधि	76a, 81
द्वादशतीर्थे पिण्डक्रिया	79, 80
धनञ्जयकोश	168b
धर्मधातुवागीश्वरमण्डलध्यान	159
[धारणीसंग्रह]	66, 67
[धारणीस्तोत्रसंग्रह]	187
धूमाङ्गरीसाधान	51d
धूमाङ्गारीपूजाविधि	68, 69
नित्यपूजाविधि	190
नित्याचारविधि	118
निदानचिकित्सा	58
पञ्चरक्षा	14, 121, 122b
पञ्चरक्षापूजाविधि	120
पञ्चविंशतिसहस्रिकाप्रज्ञापारमिता	13
पञ्चाभिषेकविधि	119
पापपरिमोचन	123, 197
[पिण्डक्रियाविधि]	126, 127, 128
पिण्डदानार्चन	10
पूजापद्धति	167, 108
प्रज्ञापारमितास्तोत्र	129

प्रज्ञोपायविनिश्चयसिद्धि	130a
प्रव्रज्याव्रतचूडाकर्मविधि	56
फलान्नप्राशनविधि	124
बालग्रहशान्ती	20
बुद्धगीत	31
बोधिचर्यावतार	25
बोधिचर्यावतारपञ्जिका	26-27
भीमरथक्रिया	23
भीमरथावरारोहणकर्म	24, 57a
भीमविनोदचिकित्सा	22
मञ्जुश्रीपाराजिका(?)	112c
मञ्जुश्रीनामसङ्गीति	11, 15, 115, 116
[मन्त्रधारणी]	113
महाप्रत्यङ्गिरामहाविद्याराज्ञी	131a
महाबलिक्रिया	107
महामण्डलेश्वरदर्शण	152, 155
महामेघमहायानसूत्र	109, 122a
महायानसूत्रालंकार	111
महासिन्दूरार्चनविधि	183
यज्ञविधि	199
यन्त्रया रक्षा	94
योगिनीविजयस्तव	200
रञ्जनालिपि	133
रत्नन्यासाविधि	134
रात्रिदिग्पूजा	16
रात्रिपूजा	135
लङ्कावतारसूत्र	105
वज्रधातुमुखाख्यान	163

वज्रवाराही देगुली	195
वज्रवाराहीमण्डलपूजा	196
[वज्रवाराहीयोगविधि]	165
वज्रवाराहीसमाधि	164
वसुधाराधारणी	166
वीरकुशावदान	198
शाक्यसिंहस्तोत्र	76b
शान्तिकमण्डलाग्नियज्ञविधान	146
श्रुतबोध	168a
षट्पारमितास्तोत्र	64
षोडशपिण्डविधि	125
संक्षिप्तक्रियाविधि	141
संक्षिप्तगुह्यपूजा	140
संक्षिप्तपिण्डक्रिया	150
संक्षिप्तबोधिचित्तोत्पाद	139
संक्षिप्तबौद्धस्तोत्रसंग्रह	138
संक्षिप्तलक्षचैत्यरचितव्रतविधि	103
सप्तशतसहस्राादिपूजा	184
समाधि	137
सम्पुटतन्त्र	89
सम्यक्दानपूजाविधि	144
सम्यक्दानराजनिमन्त्रणविधि	145
सम्वरोदयतन्त्र	143, 160
सहस्राहुतियज्ञविधि	136
सितातपत्रानामापराजितामहाविद्याराज्ञी	132
सिन्दूरपूजाविधि	149
सिन्दूरारोहनपूजा	147
सिन्दूरारोहनपूजाविधि	148
सुखावतीव्यूह	176

सुखावतीव्यूहमहायानसूत्र 110
सुगतजन्मरत्नावदानमाला 104
सुवर्णप्रभासोत्तमसूत्र 178, 179, 180
सुविक्रान्तविक्रामिपरिपृच्छा प्रज्ञापारमिता 181
सूर्यपूजाविधि 177
[स्तोत्रमन्त्रसंग्रह] 174
[स्तोत्रसंग्रह] 12, 21, 30, 142, 161, 169, 170, 171, 172, 173, 175
स्वयंभूपुराणोद्धृतबुद्धगीत 29
हेवज्रनैरात्मापूजा 93b

Manuscript Samples

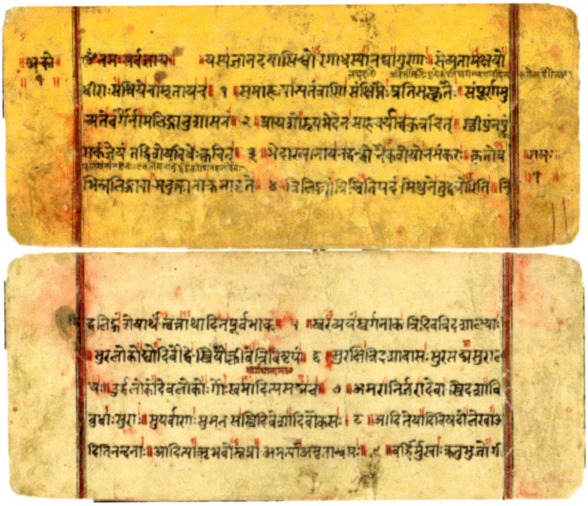

No. 9: *Amarakoṣa.* Unbounded paper, 170 folios, 5 lines/pages, complete, Devanagari script, Sanskrit and Newar (translation). Akṣeśvara Mahāvihāra (Vācaspati Vajrācārya collection) No. 63. Dated NS 1012.

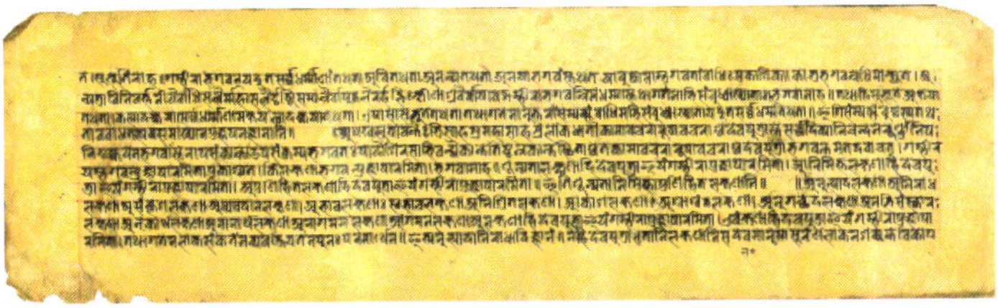

No. 13: *Pañcaviṃśatisahasrikāprajñāpāramitā.* Unbounded paper, 543 folios, 9 lines/page, complete, Pracalita script, Sanskrit.

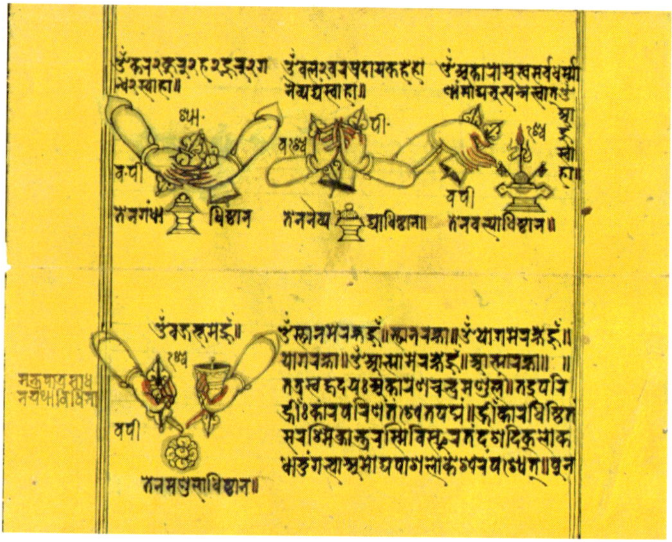

No. 18: *Amoghapāśalokeśvarapujāvidhi (Astamivratavidhi)*. Folding book, 56 folios, 6 lines/page, complete, Pracalita script, Sanskrit. Akṣeśvara Mahāvihāra (Śukrarāja Vajrācārya collection) No. 22. Illustrated.

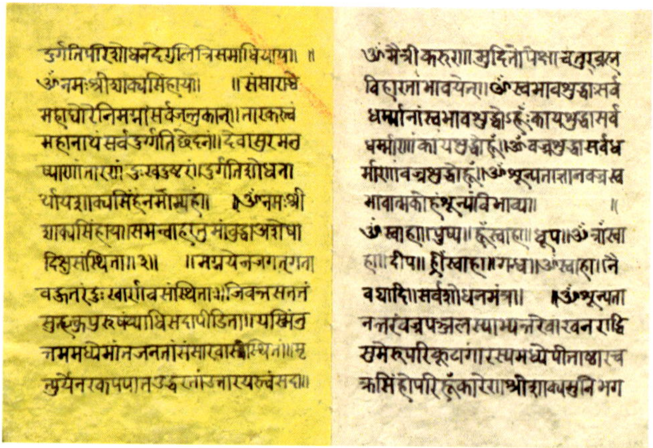

No. 74: *Durgatimaṇḍalapūjā*. Bound book, 33 (?) folios, 12 lines/page, complete, Devanagari script, Sanskrit and Newar, Akṣeśvara Mahāvihāra (Śukarāja Vajrācārya collection) No. 34.

No. 90: *Guhyasamājatantra*. Unbound paper, 168 folios, 5 lines/page, complete, Pracalita script, Sanskrit. Ratnakājī Vajrācārya collection (in the possession of Sarvajñaratna). Dated NS 830. Illustrated.

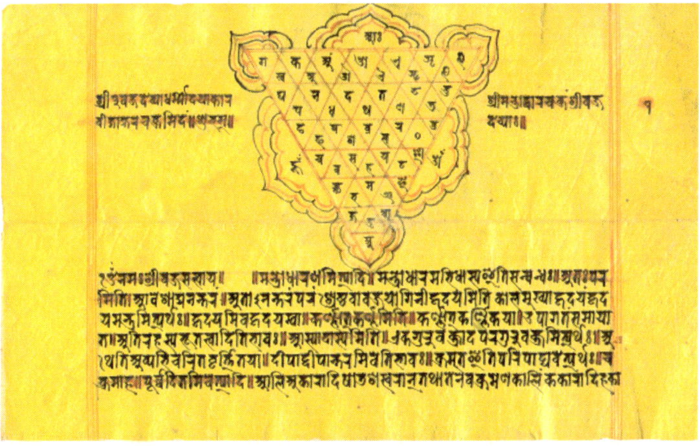

No. 114: *Tattvajnañāsaṃsiddhipañjikā Marmakālikā* by Vīryaśrīmitra (mantroddhara chapter). Unbound paper, 6 folios, 6 lines/page, complete, Pracalita script, Sankrit. Akṣeśvara Mahāvihāra collection No. 161. Illustrated.

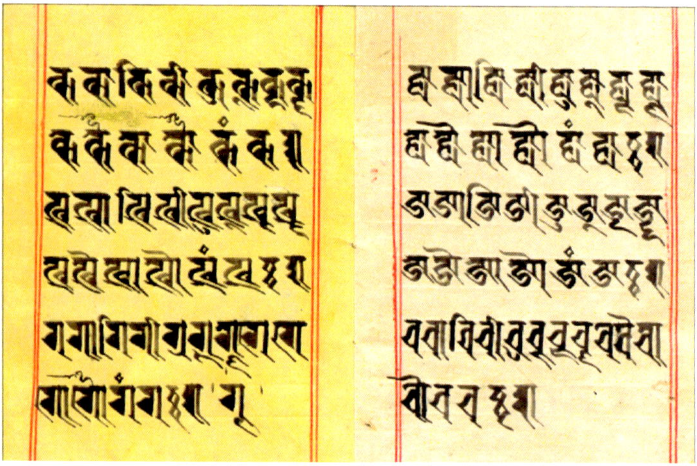

No. 133: *Rañjanālipi*. Bound book, 15 folios, 4-7 lines/page, complete, Rañjanā script, Sanskrit. Akṣeśvara Mahāvihāra (Śukrarāja Vajrācārya collection) No. 116.

No. 178: *Suvarṇaprabhāsottamasūtra*. Unbound paper, 137 folios, 5 lines/ page, 13.1 x 8.3 cm., complete, Pracalita script, Sanskrit. Dīpak Vajrācārya collection. Dated NS 878. Illustrated.

No. 179: *Suvarṇaprabhāsottamasūtra*. Unbound paper, 92 folios (numbered 1-27, 1-12, 1-12, 1-7, 1-11, 1-12, 1-12), 7 lines/page, complete, Pracalita script, Sanskrit. Akṣeśvara Mahāvihāra (Vācaspati Vajrācārya collection) No. 25. Illustrated.